How To Turn Your Website Into A Customer Getting Machine

By
John B. McDonald

Table of Contents

About John

John has 20 years' experience in the Information Technology field. 10 of those years working with small business owners to create their web presence and help to leverage the power of the Internet to attract new customers, automatically nurture relationships and educate prospects until they are ready willing and able to buy.

Introduction

Business owners today are overwhelmed with the amount of platforms they should be on to grow their business, from Facebook to Twitter to Instagram to Pinterest, the list goes on. However, most business owners are so busy servicing the needs of the clients they already have, that they are simply too busy to think about maintaining their website.

With changes to how websites are ranked according to mobile accessibility, business owners risk being left behind if their website does not stay relevant.

Website viewing numbers that will surprise you:

- There are *6 Billion* active mobile phone accounts worldwide, soon there will be fifteen billion mobile devices online.
- 91% of Americans use a mobile phone.
- A-B testing shows mobile phone advertising has a click rate ten times that of traditional browser advertising.
- More people browse the web on their mobile devices than computers, and are six times more likely to make a purchase using their mobile device.

Most websites can be optimized to automatically adapt for mobile device browsing. This is known as a responsive web design and makes navigating or reading your website a much easier experience for your customers.

If your site is not optimized for mobile viewing, you run the risk of losing out on business from people who can't find you, and it could get worse.

If you have ever thought that you're just a small business and don't need a website, think again.

- 63% of Americans *no longer* use a phone book.
- Use of the Yellow Pages has dropped a staggering 55% since 1999 and plummets a further 4% every year.

- 92% of searches for a new business start online.
- 97% of consumers use the internet to research a new product or service they are interested in.
- Over 30% of searches are for businesses in the users local area, and include the location.
- 73% of online research is for information relating to the users local community.
- 82% of searches for local businesses end in a purchase.
- More than 1.8 billion people are active users of Facebook and Twitter.

As you can see, **having an online presence is essential**. However, less than 50% of small businesses have a website, and surprisingly half of small businesses in America spend less than 10% of their advertising budget on online marketing campaigns.

Unfortunately, many business owners don't realize how much business they are missing out on because they haven't yet grasped the importance of online marketing.

So what does this mean for your business?

The website ranked #1 on Google receives 42% of all search traffic.

If you're not receiving this new business, your competition is!

Consider this: A mind-boggling 40% of internet users search for local businesses only to find they don't have a website.

If people in your area are using Google to search for a business like yours, but can't find you, they will end up doing business with your competitors.

The great news is that by creating an online presence that is optimized to increase your visibility in local search results, you can quickly and easily become visible to customers who are already looking for businesses just like yours.

Why should you use online marketing for your business?

Many small businesses favor more traditional forms of advertising such as TV, radio, or an advert in the local newspaper, meaning online advertising and local search marketing is often overlooked.

By taking advantage of this powerful yet often inexpensive form of advertising, you position yourself as the local expert in your niche which will see a steady increase in the number of customers coming to you for your product or service.

We have spoken to too many business owners who have poured thousands and thousands of dollars into TV and radio campaigns but have no way of tracking the success or failure of these campaigns.

They continue to have peaks and troughs in their business, with no real way of knowing if they are receiving a return on investment for their advertising dollar.

The reason traditional advertising forms no longer works is actually simple.

People no longer respond to this method of advertising, they have moved on. With 91% of Americans using mobile phones, people search for their own information now.

You may have done this yourself.

Have you ever been away on business or vacation and used your mobile phone to look for a restaurant, grocery store or hairdresser?

Advertising online is no longer an option – it is a fundamental requirement of doing business.

Advertising online has evolved from the 'if you build it they will come' mentality of creating a basic website with a sprinkling of keywords relevant to your business – it is now about being proactive and having your brand visible in the places your customers are already searching.

There are people out there who are looking for a business like yours, but don't even know you exist.

But there is good news!

With only a quarter of small businesses investing in online advertising, there is still time to establish your online presence before your competitors do.

So let's get started!

More and more frequently, business owners all over are worried about the fact that they are unable to draw in more customers because they lack certain skills, which are more related to the online marketing niche.

Having this in mind, and thinking about the complexity of the entire process, they simply become overwhelmed and fail to get started. In case you find yourself in this description, carefully read this guide, as it was made to help you.

This guide is not just for newcomers in the online marketing niche, but also for those that have some experience, but are looking to improve their knowledge and their business success.

CHAPTER 1

The Real Reason Why The Time To Dive Into Local Marketing Is Now, And How To Get Started

Recent studies revealed the fact that, on average, **94% of all consumers are actually buying products after they have thoroughly researched them online.** Another interesting fact is that 3 out of 5 people research online for places where to go shopping.

Interesting, right?

Today, researching online for a product, a service or a location is extremely common, and this is why more and more companies are interested in online marketing and developing their websites. In the end, it's good business if you know how to use it in your favor.

Obtaining advantages from online marketing means creating a perfect strategy and game plan, thus also helping you to have a great start.

Here is how you should get started:

1. Set Your Goals

There are countless benefits that you can obtain from choosing the online marketing strategy, but it is important that, at first, you are capable of focusing on a maximum of 2 objectives.

Think of what you are more interested in: generating customers for your business, obtain as many emails as possible for your weekly newsletter or attract visitors to your website.

2. Identify Your Main Target

As always, there is a set of questions you need to answer in order to obtain the much needed results. What do clients actually need? Do they satisfy their needs with one of your competitors? Have they ever purchased from you?

Offering them the products or services that they need, you also have to know details such as their location, their gender or hobbies, as all these will help you reach them much faster.

A great thing to know about online marketing is that it is not time-consuming or expensive, and for those that are really interested, it is quite simple to use.

Here are a few things to keep in mind:

- The online method of attracting clients is much cheaper that the offline method
- A new campaign can be launched immediately online; but not the same thing can be said about the offline version
- You can make different changes at any time you wish, with insignificant costs.
- The online marketing measuring tools display the results of your success in just a few seconds.

Local Marketing For Local Businesses – An In-Depth Understanding

Since the appearance of the Internet, its importance has become increasingly more significant, especially considering the fact that it helps offer information and creates a faster communication among us.

Even business owners have understood its importance, and how it can help them by allowing them to connect with customers all over the world, helping them find new suppliers or be up to date with the current trends.

When it comes to local business owners, it is actually understandable why they are not interested in using the online marketing strategy as a tool to connect with people that are not able to use their services, but, on the other hand, they should know and understand the fact that there are countless reasons why they should use the online marketing tool, even if they don't sell any product or service.

Consumer preferences are changing daily when it comes to interacting with local businesses, and what was until a few years ago the traditional marketing media, is now relying more and more on the digital segment, including online directories, websites, emails and mobile search.

Even today, the online marketing may seem a bit too confusing and complex for a local business owner that has to work with a tight budget. All this is due to the vast display of online marketing tools that are said to offer easier solutions for business owners, thus making them rethink their entire strategies.

The Internet—There Is No Escaping It

The main aspect that any business owner must understand is that the Internet is a powerful tool that will help them get informed, discover and offer. Every day, hundreds of millions of people are searching online for a place where they can spend their money.

The new generation of people, are just not that interested in discovering new businesses by searching their signs on the road. Online, they can obtain the necessary information without having to spend money on fuel or your nerves on the road.

Deciding to advertise their business online, they are actually making sure that people will get to know their products and services, and will likely be interested in learning more about them.

Research-backed Facts on the Wonders of Local Marketing

All this theory about the importance and benefits of the online marketing strategy is constantly backed up by thorough research and studies.

For example, a recent study commissioned by Oracle has revealed the fact that 89% of all consumers that are interested in a more detailed information about a certain product or service, will do a quick online search.

Another study, performed by Google and Ipsos MediaCT, has revealed the fact that 84% of the people owning a tablet and 88% of those that have smartphones, actually conduct online local searches.

As a connection to this first study, a Bright Local report released in February, showed the fact that the people that previously conducted an online search, are willing to go up to 17 minutes away from home in order to check out their search.

There are also studies that were made in order to show that the internet marketing as a much higher value than the traditional one.

A report has revealed that creating a lead with the help of the online marketing will actually cost $143, while the one through the outbound marketing costs $373, almost twice as much.

Even Hubspot has evidenced the fact that this more modern marketing instrument has a close rate of about 14.6%, while the traditional method only has 1.7%.

Another important aspect that local businesses need to keep in mind is that the internet doesn't just allow people to search for new services, products or brands, but it also offers the necessary tools to compare the offers and the prices.

They can obtain results based on the cheapest item, the most popular service, etc., anything they can think of. The internet must be used by local businesses to highlight their assets, their offers and their prices.

It is not enough that all these positive advantages and features to be discovered only by entering the store, if you are lucky enough.

All this is backed up by concrete data. For example, a Forrester Research has revealed the fact that 71% of the consumers in the U.S, are interested in seeing online the inventory of a store, and 50% of them are interested in making the purchase online, and then go to the store and pick up the package.

Another study, this time made by Brandpoint, shows that 68% of all consumers are actually searching online for information about certain businesses, before deciding to buy.

The Real Reason Why The Time To Dive Into Local Marketing Is Now, And How To Get Started

An AYTM Market Research even indicated that close to 70% of internet users in the United States compare prices and read reviews before going to an actual brick and mortar store.

Considering the fact that the Internet will only increase its importance, it is crucial that business owners interested in making a profit, take advantage of the available technology, even though they can't sell any products or services online. Their presence is absolutely important.

Although it is impossible to groom an animal from the Internet, you need to be aware of the fact that your business will not become profitable only with those that happen to pass by your store, or find you in the Yellow Pages.

CHAPTER 2

The Best Tools To Help You Get Started With Local Marketing

Okay, you are a small business owner. You know your business. You know its values. You know your customers. Chances are, however, you are not a marketing expert, at least not by trade.

Luckily, there is a host of highly effective tools available for productive marketing for small businesses, but in reality, you simply do not have the time or money or take full advantage of them all. So, what can you do to get the most out of your local marketing investment, in terms of both money and time?

Here are five useful resources, ranging from The Better Business Bureau and The Chamber of Commerce to Google and SEOs.

1. The Better Business Bureau

The Better Business Bureau (BBB) is a nonprofit organization that holds great value in their mission to encourage trust within the market and is the perfect choice for small businesses older than a year. Their website offers search functionality allowing customers to search business categories by location. They also offer two listing options.

Free listings
This allows you to link your business with a description and receive a citation. As a bonus, you will receive an A+ rating simply for claiming your business.

Accredited listings

Businesses with 10 or fewer employees pay a fee of $39.95 and businesses with 11-19 employees are charged at $63.33 to become accredited.

Why should you have your company accredited? Hypothetically, accrediting your business will instill consumer trust in your business. This is a win-win for companies as this is an easy, affordable accrediting gained at minimal effort.

2. The Chamber of Commerce

Many consumers, especially the Baby Boomers, are known to turn to the Chamber of Commerce to find businesses.

According to the research organization, The Shapiro Group, consumers are 63 percent more likely to purchase products or services from a small business if it is a member of the Chamber of Commerce.

Other than this, there are ore some other perks to joining the Chamber of commerce, namely:

- Adding your business to its online directory under the relevant category
- Displaying your business logo, description, link, contact information and photos
- Access to tools should you need to dispute negative reviews
- Access to reputation management reports

Other than the Chamber of Commerce, you can also look into other locally focused small business organizations in your city or state. Never underestimate the reach these smaller organizations can have, for example, Local First Arizona is a nonprofit organization boasting more than 2,500 members working to strengthen the economy of the Grand Canyon State.

Upon joining a local business group, potential consumers will be able to easily find your company indexed in the correct category. Although it is a passive form of local marketing, it can easily translate into new clients without the tedious legwork. Along with this, you can look forward to opportunities to participate in local events which are publicized, which will in turn boost your business.

3. Rating Sites (Yelp and Angie's List)

The advantages of these sites being a great platform to list your business, for free, with a large potential clientele cannot be overstated. They need a little care and if done correctly can ignite your business rather than extinguish it. Be mindful that that it is up to you to stay engaged and to handle customers, and their complaints, with grace.

Below you will see two examples, Yelp and Angie's List. They are both straight-forward and easy to get started on, simply list your business and engage where applicable.

Yelp

Simply list your business and a basic description. You can then track user views as well as your customers.

You can also opt for an enhanced profile with the following benefits:

- Photo slideshow, this will help your listing stand out from the crowd
- Expanded business description
- Block competitor's ads on your page
- Dashboard where you can track metrics
- Option to add an account manager

Visit http://www.yelp.com

Angie's List

Over and above enabling users to recognize and rate your business, there is an app, magazine and call center. The site impressively hosts 700-plus categories of home repair companies and health care professionals. If this applies to you, then this is the site you need to be on, for free!

Visit http://www.angieslistbusinesscenter.com

Bear in mind that there are various other listing sites available, some with niche market focus that would suit your business, and others that function within a state.

4. Google

Like most, you probably use Google daily. This indispensable search engine considers sites such as the Chamber of Commerce and the Better Business Bureau when determining search ranking, which is all the more reason to join them as your search rankings will only benefit. But there are other ways to take advantage of Google, namely, Google+ and Google My Business.

Google+

Have a business page on Google+ might not sound like such a big deal, after all, it is not a great social media platform, but it will increase your online visibility.

All it takes is a few minutes to create a page, which will in turn result in new customers and revenue. You can also add your Google+ page to your website along with your personal profile pages, which will greatly expand your overall reach.

Google My Business

Once you have established your Google+ account, sign up for the very useful Google My Business. This is a useful tool enabling you to edit your business on Google Search and to add your business to Google Maps, which will allow customers to easily locate you. This will also make your business more easily accessible as clients will be able to connect with you over a range of devices.

5. Search Engine Optimization (SEO)

Firstly, what are SEOs? Basically, they are words and phrases that help you rank higher in search engines and as such need to be relevant to your small business.

In recent times, SEO lines have been getting blurred. Proper indexing of websites and sole focus on SEO are no longer as important, yet sources such as Forbes have reported that Google still considers factors such as the number of +1s on a Google+ Business Page when determining ranking.

Google uses an algorithm which calculates search engine results based on factors such as blogs, quality content, social media presence, and the use of sites such as the Chamber of Commerce and Google+.

What does this mean for you, the small business owner? Well, you need to adhere to some simple guidelines for Search Engine Optimization and you will get good rankings on various search engines.

Here they are, according to Google's expert tips:

- Accurately describe page content
- Create unique title tags for each page
- Use descriptive titles
- Use word in URLs
- Write easy-to-read text
- Create content primarily for your users, not search engines
- Supply alternative text when using images as links

Even if your business is established and growing, do not let go of the basics. You should never feel your business to be above simple marketing techniques like registering with the local Chamber of Commerce or creating a Google+ page. A little time and effort can reap great rewards for your business.

Google, of course, is the most powerful tool that you can use to market your business online. This is why you need to focus most of your resources, effort and time into understanding how to dominate Google and to leverage it for your local business.

Read on as we go in deeper into Google and using it as your local business marketing "superpower".

CHAPTER 3

Dissecting Google Local and How It Affects You and Your Business

How is Google changing the way we do business?

If there has ever been a technology that will put your business on the map – it is Google Local. With all the hype surrounding this nifty online platform, it is time to sit up and take notice.

A Trip Down Memory Lane – How Did It All Start?

Google Local has an interesting timeline. It started as **Google Maps**, was rechristened Google Places, and then named Google Plus Local before the web giant finally found a name that suits it best – Google Local.

Google's process of creating a record was elaborate and complex. It started with a search through various sources for information about an organization. The data was then collated to form a record about the business.

This intricate procedure was well worth the effort. For a start, it helped create the most extensive and wide-ranging directory of businesses across the globe. However, that is not its best attribute – its winning feature is the fact that Google Local is a platform that provides online visibility to businesses.

Growing Pains: Challenges Of Collecting The Data

Up until three years ago, the data for Google Local came from a range of sources. These included users' dashboards, Google Map Maker, third party information and other places on the internet. This data was then pulled together in to a "cluster".

The record was reviewed every six weeks. This period accounts for a long interval in the business world – lengthy enough for organizations to change. Mergers, takeovers and sometimes even dissolution meant that the cluster became inaccurate and had to be created all over again.

Another challenge was the number of people who ended up controlling the information about a company. With several users having the ability to claim a company on their dashboard, managing the information became increasingly complex.

Eureka! Let's Do Things The Google Way

In 2012, the entire process was made much simpler by creating a canonical database for all the local listings.

This is when a new era began for Google Local, as it moved in the Knowledge Graph.

The Internet giant had now found a way to preserve its identity using a platform that it trusted. While this change did not do away with the need to tap into other sources for information, it did give Google the flexibility to build new data pipelines and interfaces so people could contribute by adding information to a particular listing.

Users have welcomed the interfaces - these include Map Maker, Places for Business Dashboard and of course Google Plus Local. What this has allowed Google to achieve is a database of local business information that is growing by the minute.

The Future: Synchronizing The Information

There is increasing evidence that Google is considering assembling the various interfaces into a single solution.

For example, a change you make in Google+ will reflect in your dashboard and vice versa. This means as with all things Google, this product is being refined constantly.

Perhaps this is why it does not come as a surprise that now there is a limit to the number of ways you can claim a listing. If you have listed yourself as the owner of a company on Google+ or Google Dashboard, then the system will not allow you to add it to another dashboard.

Your Listing Is Owned By Google

The rationale behind Google Local is to provide accurate online information about businesses. In doing so, Google trusts some sources more than others. Your business is a primary, but a single source of information.

This means it is likely that Google may use another source to update your company's listing. Do not be alarmed if you see your business' listing change – it is probably because the algorithm deemed another source more trustworthy.

Not only this, there is a chance you might see old data re-emerge. The reason for this is that Google retains information about your business over a long period of time.

Google's Goldmine: A Plethora Of Data

It is little wonder that with so many sources there may be an overabundance of data. However, this information is never superfluous for Google.

In fact, their solution is to syndicate the data to the Google's other platforms. This means all the information is distributed pretty much across a range of hardware and software.

Arguably, Google is unrelenting in this regard. Where the data may end up is not their concern, they only interest themselves with the issue of displaying data where they deem appropriate.

The Types Of Google+ Pages

Businesses have various kinds pages on Google+, a quick look at these can help recognize where an owner might be in the process of claiming a listing.

However, before understanding the nature of pages, it is important to consider how Google looks at them. No matter how sophisticated or interactive a page might be, it is ultimately a single representation of the business.

Essentially there are four types of pages.

Identifying an *unclaimed page* is rather easy, these have only two tabs at the top and there is no description from the owner. Any image that appears on such a page is what Google found on the web.

A *claimed page*, on the other hand, has information provided by the business owner. If the claimed page is from the old Dashboard, the description on it will be no longer than 200 words.

In case the page is claimed in the new Dashboard, Google + or has been upgraded to social, it may contain various types of information, including videos and social postings – if these are present the page will have more than two tabs.

There is also no limit to the number of words that can be used in the description. If a verified symbol appears on the page, it is an indication that the business can add social content to Google.

A full fledge Google Plus page is one that engages with the audience using social and video streams as well as a longer description. These pages usually have four tabs.

There Is No Place Like Home

You may think the world of your Google+ page, but chances are most users may never actually visit it. So what is the most important page for your business then?

Well, it is **Google's Search Engine Results Page (SERP)** - this is where all the action happens.

The *Knowledge panel* on the right side of the results page is where you need to focus. There is a lot of data displayed in this section - from reviews to photographs and ratings. In essence, this portion gives users the information Google thinks is most important for them.

Make sure what ends up here is presentable; this is because the knowledge panel is the face of your business. For example, if you are a recruitment business you may want to request your clients and candidates to leave some stellar reviews and ratings.

When it comes to positive feedback, opinions of people from various geographical locations add clout to your online reputation. The coveted five-star rating, too, is becoming increasingly more valuable for businesses.

Another aspect worth considering is the photograph that appears on this page. Select images carefully and ensure they represent the impression you want to create.

For instance, a spa business that promises a relaxing retreat for clients should consider including interior street view. To make sure users do not see a competitor's ad in the carousel, include your ad in the brand.

When all is said and done, what is emerging is a new model of online business visibility. The focus is shifting from Search Engine Optimization to optimizing conversion rates.

Channel Your Energies In The Right Direction

Ultimately, what matters is your relationship with Google. You have very little control over a listing, and you are a small part of their local data syndication system. Therefore, your Google+ page holds virtually no importance in the big picture. It is the main page where you need to put all the right kind of information.

Now, the next step is to start rolling our sleeves up and get down to the nitty gritty of things.

CHAPTER 4

Bring Out Your SEO Guns and Do It Like The Pros: A Step-By-Step Guide To Local SEO Marketing

Let's pretend it is the 1990s, you've moved towns and lost your glasses in the process. Now you need a new pair. What would you do?

You would pick up the Yellow Pages, turn to the relevant category, find a few optometrists close by, circle their contact details and then one by one punch their phone number on your landline to get an idea of what they have an offer.

Finally, you would shortlist some and make an appointment to get new glasses.

Sounds a bit tedious – right? Let's stick to 2015 in that case.

If you need a product or service, all you need to do is look through Google and it returns with a list of nearby vendors. The search engine has become so synonymous with making our lives simpler that we have now adopted it as a term for looking for something online. We no longer search for something, we Google it.

If you are a business, consider the flipside of the coin. At the time of the paper directories, company names were listed alphabetically. You had no sway over how far down your name would be appear. Sometimes, if your pocket allowed it, you could make your product or service stand out by including an ad, but that was pretty much it.

Luckily, Google does not rely on the alphabet to list results. It rewards websites based on the quality of their content.

So, it goes without saying, this is a great time to be in business.

Most people already know SEO can deliver marketing value. Local search is a part of SEO and if you are wondering how you can optimize your website benefit from it, you have come to the right place.

This is the first installment of a series of posts that are aimed at helping you make the most of local search engine marketing.

Before we delve into how you can improve your online visibility, let's start with understanding the nature of the market place.

The Profile Of The Modern Customer

We are in the midst of a digital revolution. The landscape has changed with developments that take place on a daily basis.

A whopping 125 million people in the United States alone have a smartphone—a figure that makes up more than half the mobile subscribers in the country.

Let's now look at how these smartphone owners use their devices for local search:

- Around five in 10 use their smart phone to search for local information
- Three in 10 are willing to scan a mobile tag for coupons
- Close to half will research a product on their phone before making a purchase

Local search is becoming an essential part of our daily lives. How many times you have searched for a keyword followed by the city you are in? This is because you know that the results with a local search will be more relevant.

For example, searching for "library New York" will deliver more suitable results compared to the term "library" alone.

Here is a breakdown of how users are researching local businesses:

- A colossal 4 billion queries from desktop computers in the United States have local intent.
- Half of all mobile searches are looking for local results.
- Every fifth search is on mobile

Based on this data, experts concluded that approximately seven billion unique local searches take place on a monthly basis and the United States.

Understanding The Basics

Local search has three building blocks:

- Local Listings and Citations
- Online Reviews
- On-Site Local SEO optimization

Local Listings and Citations

The Internet has thousands of platforms where you can list your business.

Customers today are inundated with choices; the marketplace is bursting at the seams with options. From eateries to real estate, every product or service has several businesses vying for their attention.

Search engines make it easier for customers to make an informed decision. This is because they allow users to enter keywords and return with results that appear in order of quality and consumer preference.

Based on how relevant and useful the results are, users decide which search engine to use in the future. Since search engines are able to monetize on advertising, they use algorithms to produce the most appropriate results.

This means massive amounts of data needs to be processed to be able to return the most relevant options sorted by geographical location. Google is a great example of a search engine that refined its algorithm to produce the best results.

Understanding Local Listings

The next question is how search engines ensure that superior quality of data. They do so by cross-referencing each data point through various sources on the web. Popular names such as Google and Bing rely on three major data brokers.

These are: Infogroup, Axciom and Neustar Localeze.

The data provided by this trio is then cross-checked against popular business listing services like Google+ Local, Yelp, Bing Places, Yellow Pages, Yahoo Local and Foursquare.

Essentially, if a business listing is consistent across multiple data providers it becomes more trustworthy and hence more likely to turn up in search engine results. The bottom line is quality and relevance are rewarded.

There are ways you can boost your online presence with local business listings.

Think of the business listing as your profile online. With thousands of websites and directories allowing businesses to create these for free, the Internet is full of details about businesses from all around the world.

As part of your marketing strategy try to create as many consistent business listings as possible to increase your online visibility. This allows for various crosscheck points hence adding credibility to your listing. Ultimately, this boosts the likelihood of ranking well in local searches.

There are three components of a quality business listing.

These are:

1. *A business name that is consistent across the web:* You may think this one is a no-brainer. However, it is easy to make a mistake.

   For example, if your business is called Bill's Accounting Services in one place and Bill Accountants in another listing, search engines will view these as separate businesses. Staying consistent across all directories is essential.

2. A local phone number that matches your city. This cannot be shared for number, a toll-free number or a call tracking number.

3. A dedicated physical street address. Again, this cannot be a shared address, PO Box all virtual office.

In addition to the above criteria, it is also a good idea to be mindful of the following:

- Make sure the title of your listing reflects your business's actual title.
- Including a descriptor is a good idea – it tells users where you are and what your business offers
- Make sure the descriptor does not include marketing taglines, phone numbers, store codes or URLs
- Do not add superfluous keywords to your business name
- New businesses can benefit from having a name that describes your services as well as location. For example, Joe's New York Pizza
- If you are an existing business and have a registered name, but it does not contain the keywords you want to include, you could register a new Doing Business As (DBA) name. However, remember consistency across listings is crucial.

Describing The Nature Of Your Business

Search engines usually allow businesses to place their listing in up to five categories.

These help determine the nature of the business. Data from this field helps the algorithm pick which listing to show for a search.

Uncategorized listings are likely to be penalized by the search engine. Incorrectly categorized listings are also not favored.

The Moz Local Category Research Tool is quite helpful when choosing categories for your listing.

What is a citation?

A citation is a mention of business profile on a page other than your own. It includes your address and/or phone number and may include your website as well.

Citations add excellent value to your online presence. This is because search engines have two ways to rank your listing - by visiting the links that point to your website, and tracking sites where those links appear.

Businesses with high quality links as well as citations of credible websites tend to be rewarded by algorithms.

For example, a business that is mentioned on the Chamber of Commerce website and includes a link to it will rank quite high.

The moral of the story is that make sure you list your company's details in as many places on the web as possible.

When it comes to getting citations there are a number of avenues to explore:

- You could contact various credible local websites yourself and get them to include your details.
- There is the option of signing up with an agency that specializes in creating an online presence.
- Invest in a location-based Content Management System. All you need to do is upload your address and the software will push your listing to various locations. There are several CMS options available – some of these are Yext, Moz Local and UBL. Investigate each alternative to purchase the CMS that suits your needs perfectly.

Online Reviews

It is said word-of-mouth is the most potent form of marketing. In today's world this is truer than ever before.

Research suggests around eight in 10 customers say online reviews are like personal recommendations to them. More than half say they become more open dealing with a local business if there is positive online feedback for them.

While views are divided in regards to search engine rankings based on reviews, it is certain that customers look at opinions to make a decision.

It is imperative that you engage your client base. This is especially true for your best customers; positive reviews will add to your trustworthiness online.

Similarly, when a customer has left a criticism of your product or service online ask them what made them feel that way. It is important you find out what you can do to change their opinion.

Remember, reviewing platforms have their own set of guidelines. Google and Yelp are particularly specific in terms of their review policies. Make sure your customers adhere to these guidelines and you will derive the positive outcome you are looking for.

A higher click through rate to your website is an obvious advantage of online reviews. However, studies suggest that the depth and breadth of views on your listing also affects your business' visibility on the search engine page results.

Online reputation management is becoming increasingly critical for small businesses. Do not feel apprehensive about inviting people to give you online feedback.

You can do so by including a call to action at a key spot on your website. For example, the checkout page is a great place to ask people for a review. You could also bring it up in a face-to-face conversation that you may have with a customer.

Researchers argue that the volume of reviews as well as their diversity play a crucial role in helping algorithms determine the integrity of your listing.

Go Visual To Get Clicks

Analytics point to the fact that images and videos increase the number of clicks a listing may get. In fact, this is a great way to showcase your offering. If you want to stand out, go visual.

However, your ranking is not affected by photos and videos, customers on the other hand are more susceptible to listings with images.

Remember to choose images wisely. Try is much as possible to use photographs to engage the customer.

Social Factors

Social media has taken the Internet landscape by storm. This means that the social element of SEO is gradually gaining stronger foothold.

Review oriented social platforms such as Google + allow businesses to communicate with their followers. This is especially useful in responding to feedback.

Other Attributes

There are certain factors that businesses tend to overlook. As a result, their listing is penalized by search engines. One such mistake is not using the correct format to enter your complete contact information. If any details are not in an *indexable* text, chances are they will be missed out by search engines. Do not embed important information in an image, Flash or any other layout that a search engine cannot crawl.

If you prefer not to include your contact details, set up a contact us page which displays your company's name, physical address and phone numbers. This basic information is abbreviated as NAP. To enhance the performance of your NAP code it in schema, which is a markup code that all key search engines understand.

The physical location of your local business may influence how you rank.

Make sure you follow the policies of any platform where you will include your listing. **Comply with the guidelines to avoid penalty**. Breaches can lead to a negative impact on your rankings, worse yet your listing could even be removed from the index.

As discussed earlier, stay consistent in terms of the data that is published about your business at various locations. Last but not least, **keep up with the changes in policy** and keep an eye out for any promotion opportunities that may pop up. Following these basic steps is a great way to ensure that you rank high online and in the minds of your customers.

CHAPTER 5

The Real Deal on Getting Listed and Ranked on Google Local Listings

Thankfully, most small business owners know all too well the importance of online marketing. In my experience, it is a vital component of the marketing mix, and while there are many ways to get noticed on the internet, the best way to get online attention, has always been Google.

Because of its ever-reaching virtual arm, a business owner would be well-advised to take advantage of Google's local business-focused Google Places.

Google Places is free and easy to set up and is a 'must-have' tool for any locally focused business. This article is going to take you through the simple steps of exactly how to get your business listed on Google Places and more importantly, it's going to take you through the task of getting ranked.

Account Setup and Getting Listed

Firstly (and before we get to optimization), I am going to take you through a step-by-step process of getting your business listed on Google Places. The initial setup is simple, straightforward, and the process shouldn't take longer than an hour.

Step 1 – Create a Google Account for Your Business

Let's start with the basics; you're going to need a Google account for your business. Like most people, you probably already have a personal

Google account, but it is advisable to make another one specifically for your business.

There are a few reasons for this: at some point there is the probability that an employee will manage your business listing, and you certainly don't want them posting and perusing your personal account.

Keeping accounts separate is also necessary should your business ever be sold or switch hands in the future. Try to keep your business account easy to remember. Most people will simply setup their business name @gmail.com.

Step 2 – Claim Your Business as Yours

Once your business Gmail account is good to go, then you can claim your business and get it listed on Google Places. Go to the (G Places) homepage and click **"Get Started"**. Once you've clicked "**Get your business found on Google**", you're A for away.

You will more than likely have to search for your business by country and phone number, as this is the first time you're listing your business under a business account. It is important at this stage that you use the business landline for this search otherwise Google won't recognize your business (because of the Google maps integration).

When you search for your business, Google will do the following: it will either find your business or reveal your basic information (usually pulled from Yell or other such directory sources), or it will take you to the next step covered under "Step 3": Edit Your Business Listing (below).

How's it possible that I've already been listed? What happens now? The good news here is that the information you add will be able to be edited and more information about your business can be added later, so don't stress! At this point your business is simply being claimed as yours and you'll now move on to the essential part of this guide.

Step 3 – Edit Your Business Listing

You are now in control of your listing and can get started on customizing and capturing all your business details. Prepare yourself, there is quite a lot of information that needs entering and Google will want you to be very specific. Don't panic, we're here to give you a good idea of how to be efficient in each section.

Basic Information

The Basic Information is easy to understand and, you guessed it, where you'll capture all of the basics of your business. This section is very important for your listing.

Here are the categories, directly from Google, that your listing must have:

- Country
- Company Name
- Address
- City, County, Postcode
- Main Phone Number

Google wants to trust your business and make things as simple as possible for the consumer, so while the fields are pretty self-explanatory, what's important to note here, is that consistency is key, so capture everything the same as how you've done in the past.

Double-check other websites that your business is on, (Qype or FreeIndex), and make sure that every detail is identical. Pay attention to detail here because even the simplest thing like using St. instead of Street can make a difference to Google.

Another important aspect of your listing is your "business description" in "Basic Information". You'll have 200 (or less) characters to make your business shine. Perhaps address it as something that you would feature on your business website. Be sure to use keywords that accurately target the description to your ideal consumers/customers.

Service Areas and Location Setting Areas

Here, you'll have the opportunity of displaying your business in one location or if it does business in multiple locations. If your business does not do outside business or deliveries, then simply select that one location option and you're done.

If your business operates in multiple locations, then you'll have to determine the area of service. You can either provide a delivery distance from your location or list the cities and/or areas that you want to be listed in. Both of these options have their advantages and it all depends on the type of your business.

Hours of Operation and Payment Options

In this section (which is also pretty straight-forward), Google will automatically retrieve the required information from your company website if you don't enter it, so be sure to avoid any errors or misinformation by entering the information yourself.

In order to build your reputation with Google and to ensure trustworthiness, be sure to fill everything out as completely and in as much detail (without being boring) as possible.

Images/Photos

Images are a very important part of your listing and should definitely be included. Brand conscious photos will make your business appear attractive to potential customers. They will also make you look more professional and trustworthy, especially on Google.

Be careful though - you are limited to 10 images, so be sure to use your best possible pictures, depicting your brand accurately. It's also a good idea to list your most important pictures first, so that customers see your best ones even if they don't look through them all.

Your pictures should include:

- Company logo
- Images of your employees at work/your business
- Images of your products
- Images of the business itself

Videos

Videos aren't really necessary in your listing, but as long as they are short and professional, definitely won't hurt. Each and every well-branded visual aid added, builds credibility and displays trustworthiness.

Additional Details

It might be tempting to put extra marketing and keywords in this section, but I don't suggest that you do. The best use of this area is to list the things similar to the examples that Google offers (parking on site, brands carried).

Keywords can be used in the other sections, but reserve this area for important details that couldn't fit in other areas.

Step 4 – Verify Your Google Places Listing

You're almost done! You'll need to verify with Google that you do actually own your business before you can take full control of your listing. Verifying procedure - there are two options for verifying: either by phone or mail. Snail-mail verification can take 2-3 weeks, so you'll want to use the phone (mobile/landline) option. (This option is available in 99% of cases).

Immediately once you choose the phone option, your business line will receive an automated call from Google. This will give you a 5-digit verification pin. Enter the pin and you're ready to go.

Optimizing Your Google Places Listing

While your business is all set up and verified on Google Places, there are still some things that can be done to get the highest-possible ranking on your listing.

Being listed is a good start, but being found is crucial and whilst we've covered a few little tricks above, we need to go through a few more good practices to help you get your rankings up.

Maintain Google Places Listing

This might seem obvious, but you will want to keep updating your page and changing any details as and when they happen. It's also a good idea to check the analytics on your website and adapt your listing accordingly until you get the required traffic from it.

Market Your Google Places Listing

Giving your listing some love and attention, even though it may seem redundant to market a marketing tool, will really make a big difference in the long run.

Consider these steps to ensure that your Google Places listing gets the most attention possible:

- Use transactional emails and mailing lists to encourage your customers to review your listing.
- Use your Google Places page to post updates regarding coupons and discounts
- Use other review service platforms to build up business reviews
- Optimize your business website for Google

Utilize Citations to Improve Your Google Ranking

The last thing that we're going to cover which is guaranteed to help your ranking, is the all important tool of citations. Google loves to see your business being mentioned on other websites, so having a good list of third party citations is one of the best things you can do to improve your local ranking.

There are numerous services that list local businesses. Getting yours on just a few of these (especially the right ones) will certainly help you in your pursuit of getting noticed by the right customers. A great starting place would be LocalVisibilitySystem, to see the types of websites that

CHAPTER 6

Maximizing Your Google Places Visibility—Getting Better Reviews for Your Local Business

How do customers know that your business is trustworthy and reputable?

Third party customer reviews and testimonials have always been essential and very effective to demonstrate that your business "walks the talk", and with local search services like Google Places prominently displaying reviews, they've become more important than ever.

The problem most people/businesses face is getting consistent, authentic reviews and testimonials, as these require an approach that is proactive and that encourages positive customer engagement with their profile.

The great news is that reviews provide multi-channel retailers with invaluable and relevant feedback about their products and services. When used to your advantage, they are an excellent marketing tool that can motivate new customers to visit your online store, website or even physical retail location.

More exposure equals more potential reviews and sales.

Where to start?

Let's help you get better Google Places reviews for your business.

Google Places for Business

Google Places for Business is a local advertising and marketing service that connects shoppers with local businesses that sells products relevant to their shopper's requirements.

The service allows any business with a physical location to display store information such as location, images, video-clips, specials and more.

Your Google Places profile will also include authentic customer-submitted reviews. These reviews should reflect an honest experience about a retailer's service, product, price, quality, and general trustworthiness of their store.

They're also the perfect opportunity to demonstrate positive social feedback for your business.

So, a shopper who is not familiar with a local retail shop can use these reviews to base their decision on whether or not to visit the store at all.

Pretty powerful, right?

It is for this reason that marketers should try to encourage shoppers to publish Google Places reviews.

It's pretty simple when you have the right information. Here are 4 ways to do just that.

1. Ask For A Review After Their Transaction

Once a customer has made a purchase from either you, online or in-store, ask that customer to provide you with feedback about the products purchased, service provided and any improvements required in order to make future shopping more effective.

In-store, this may include handing the shopper a receipt with the Google Places review box URL printed on it or in a scan-able format that they can simple scan into with their smart-phones at their convenience.

For an online store, consider including the review request in an email a week or so later, after the client has received the order. At the bottom of a shipping notification email could also be appropriate.

2. Link Directly to the Review Form

Remember that convenience is always key, so a smart strategy for driving more reviews is to point visitors directly to the Google Places review form as opposed to providing a URL that sends them to your general Google Place page.

Ideally a business should integrate Google Places with Google+ (this is an important step toward optimizing a Places profile for search), so the target review URL will be similar to this:

https://plus.google.com/GOOGLE_IDENTIFIER_GOES_HERE /about?gl=US&hl=en-US&review=1

This link can be used on websites, in advertising and marketing promotions, and any time a customer is asked to leave a review. Of course, the link can be shortened and customized via bit.ly

3. Show Off Positive Reviews

Most people enjoy being part of a group – they enjoy recognition from that group. Studies have shown that the desire for group acknowledgement is the underlying psychological reason why people write positive reviews.

Take pride in displaying or "showing off" your positive Google Places reviews. They are important - include them on your website, at checkout in the physical store and in select offers and promotions.

For example, a merchant might produce a video showing various positive reviews set to upbeat music. This attention may invite and encourage new customers to join the shoppers praising that very store.

4. Reward Reviews After Given

Most people value the opinions of friends, family and relatives. They are trustworthy, right? Google Places reviews are a form of word-of-mouth marketing, where customers are effectively telling potential customers that a store and/or product is trustworthy.

Word-of-mouth marketing can make or break a business – always encourage service excellence and reward reviewers for their shopping experience.

As an example, consider rewarding a regular shopper who writes a positive review on your Google Places page with a free t-shirt, a special discount, or some other gift, the next time they shop or visit your store.

For online shoppers leaving positive reviews, the merchant could consider emailing the reviewer free shipping on future orders or free merchandise with their next purchase. In each case the rewarded reviewer is more likely to tell friends, who in turn could write their own reviews.

Be Cautionary When Requesting A Review

As a general rule of being authentic, any kind of reward should be unexpected and given after the shopping experience, as point number four above suggests. Shoppers shouldn't be offered a chance to win a gift or reward for writing a review.

Offering a reward for a review afterwards is very different to promising a gift before a shopper reviews their store.

The former is doing something nice for a customer that has taken action of their own accord. The latter, offering a reward in advance, may be seen as a bribe and unethical for writing what some critics have called false/fake reviews.

One such case that received enough significant negative attention to have lost the opportunity to market in the Amazon Marketplace, VIP Deals, when in January 2012, after the New York Times reported that the company had been refunding their customers who wrote positive reviews.

VIP Deals unfortunately went a bit further than most companies, and this case soured the general practice of exchanging reviews for offers and actioning any review given under these circumstances as "fake."

Dealing With Negative Reviews

Having a plan for managing any negative reviews that come in via Google Places is important as the final consideration for encouraging positive Google Places reviews.

Once your Google Places for Business account is connected with your Google+ account, you publicly access the ability to respond to reviews. So when a negative review does come in, you have the opportunity to tactfully correct any inaccuracies and offer solutions to any problem.

Remember, customers need to believe that if something does go wrong with the purchase process, your business is attentive and that you will make an effort to fix things.

Remember too, that legitimate negative reviews are ways for you to reassess and improve upon within your business, either personal or system improvement.

CHAPTER 7

Leveraging Social Media to Dominate Your Local Market

When small business owners think marketing, they think social media. These days most business owners already have several personal social media accounts to keep in contact with family and friends, so it feels like a natural progression to try and grow their business through these channels as well.

The problems can start when business owners take a scattergun approach to social media, setting up accounts on Facebook, Twitter, Pinterest, Instagram and the rest, and using them all badly.

Without focus or structure, and without a firm understanding of how to grow or interact with their followers, they set themselves up for failure.

Social media is as the name suggests, for socializing. It is a place to start a conversation and engage with current or potential customers. Think of it like a weekend get together with friends, and you are the host. Friends aren't visiting you so you can sell them timeshare, they enjoy your company.

Your followers are the same, they follow you as a source of information, not to have pressure to buy your product shoved in their faces every time you post.

Engage your followers by asking what they need help with, what you can do to solve their problems, and what they would like to hear more about. Make them feel like they are a part of your community and your business. By doing this, you avoid only talking about yourself or your business.

Time is money, so you need to ensure you spend your time wisely. That means spending time on the social media platforms that your customers are on. Just because you love Twitter doesn't mean your customers do.

Think of your target audience and research the platforms they use to give your social media campaign the perfect start.

How do you do that? Ask them! How do you do that? Asking at the counter in your store is a great way, as is an email survey to your distribution list.

We have put together a guide for each major social media platform to assist you to build and engage with followers for your local business.

Make The Most Of Your Time On Facebook

Watching viral videos is fun, but it won't help you grow your business.

With more than 71% of American adults using Facebook, this social media behemoth puts their competitors such as Twitter and Pinterest in the shade.

As a result, many business owners believe that a critical factor in their online success is to have a large Facebook presence. This can be true for many businesses, but it is all relative to the amount of time you want to spend building your online community.

Thanks to the constant changing nature of Facebook algorithms, posts from business pages are only seen by approximately 2.5% of the brands followers. As a result, a vast majority of business owners only see a small financial return on their time investment, and some even see zero return.

This may be because Facebook is not known as the best channel for acquiring customers. If your main social media goal is quantity of followers, then Twitter or Instagram may be better suited to your needs.

Facebook could then be used to serve the purpose it was created for: Building brand loyalty and turning your online community into spokespeople for your brand.

Use Twitter To Grow Your Business Locally

There are more than 200 million people actively using Twitter, and a quarter of those users are in the United States. So while it is much smaller than Facebook, it is still a highly used and highly influential platform. Twitter is incredibly popular with people on the move, as 75% of its users use their mobile device to interact.

Twitter can be like attending a networking event where if you want to, you can listen in on everyone's conversations.

However, there are some golden rules:

1. Networkers who only talk about themselves become boring, fast.

2. If you're new to networking events, it can be difficult to find people to connect with.

3. If you're not on the ball, you could miss out on a perfect opportunity

The second two points are the biggest reasons local business owners struggle to grow their business via Twitter successfully.

However, there is no cause for alarm, as we have some quick tips to get you going in the right direction.

Create An Account On Twitter

First things first, you will need to visit http://twitter.com and create an account. Choose a username that is specific to your business, unique to you, relevant, and short.

People remember short account names easier, and with only 140 characters available per tweet, it leaves customers more characters to play with when they want to connect with you.

Your username should also be consistent with the username you have chosen on other social media platforms, if possible.

Fill in all the information on the profile page in a way that will pique the interests of your audience, and include as much information as possible: Logo, business description, link to your website or landing page and a background image that is relevant to your product or service.

Follow People

Many of your friends, family, and business contacts may already be on Twitter.

Following them gives you a great list of people you can jump into conversations with. Many mobile devices also give you the option of searching through your phones contact list to see who has a Twitter account, and automatically follow them for you.

Another way to find people to follow is through third party software. A great one is called www.crowdfireapp.com as it has a function called 'copy followers'.

This allows you to enter the account names of your competitors, and follow the people who follow them. These people will be more likely to follow you as they are already interested in a similar product or service to what you are offering.

Thirdly there is an Advanced Search option in Twitter which allows you to get really specific. Enter a keyword for your niche or a keyword for something you know your target customers are interested in, and select the 'Near This Place' option. This will give you a highly targeted list of accounts to follow.

Find A Twitter Management App

Unlike Facebook, Twitter is much easier to use through third-party apps and is actively encouraged. It also offers time efficiencies such as the ability to schedule tweets.

Two excellent apps are Tweetdeck and Hootsuite. Both apps allow you to filter people into categories such as customers, prospective customers, important people and influencers in your industry. Both apps also let you schedule tweets and set up notifications for when someone direct message or @mentions you.

For Twitter on the go, the mobile app for Apple or Android is also a must.

Watch And Listen Then Talk

It's exciting to see your favorite influencer or celebrity crush on Twitter, we get that. A great idea is to watch and learn, listening for the tone of conversations, getting an idea of peoples interests and how they like to interact.

If you see something you like, give it a retweet before launching in with your opinion.

Think First Then Tweet

As you get to understand the idiosyncrasies of Twitter, the associated apps, and the tone of the people you follow, dive in and start tweeting yourself.

There are no strict rules, but a general rule is 33% tweets, 33% replies or retweets and 33% links to your website and self-promotion.

People aren't robots, so they respond better to tweets that show who you are as a person and give potential customers an opportunity to get to know you. Doing this will help to gain the trust of your followers.

If someone @mentions you, replies to a tweet, or retweets something you tweeted make an effort to thank that person straight away, then start a conversation with them. Accounts that have a high engagement rate are more successful, as a key ingredient to social media is being social.

Entice Followers

Unfortunately, there is no guaranteed formula to entice people to follow you. Like most things in life, and especially in online marketing and brand building, it takes hard work and dedication.

But fear not, as we have five tips to get your Twitter engagement soaring and follower numbers increasing.

1. Use offline and online methods to promote your Twitter account.

Put up a Twitter logo with your @handle in your store so people can find you. Add a link to your Twitter account in your email signature.

2. Offer discounts specific to Twitter.

This can be an excellent way to get your account seen by more eyeballs as discounts, giveaways or competitions are much more likely to spread virally than a standard tweet.

3. Show people what you do with photos.

If you're a flower arranger, show a beautiful wedding bouquet. If you're a restaurant, show the incredible desserts your guests will be eating that night.

If you're a personal trainer, show your clients enjoying themselves in the sunshine. Photos give a visual representation of what you do and offer a chance to inject your personality into your account. They are also a lot more interesting than a link to your lead magnet.

4. Start a conversation.

Ask your network questions about things going on in your community, ask for their opinion, find out what their problem is and how you can solve it.

If you're visiting a new city, ask for restaurant recommendations or the best place to get coffee.

5. Offer customer service through Twitter.

This can be a powerful way to interact with your customers as it lets you address issues quickly, but be careful. If you can't respond to tweets within five to ten minutes you risk angering your customer further, so Twitter may not be the best platform for these interactions.

Also avoid trading hostilities. If a conversation is going down a path you don't feel comfortable with, pick up the phone and deal with the issue directly.

Build A Pinterest Following

Pinterest has exploded onto the scene receiving 10 million unique visitors per month in a little under two years, making it one of the fastest-growing websites of all time.

Throw in the fact that over 50% of all interactions happen on mobile devices and you have a perfect candidate for a place to create a local network of fans.

Below are some suggestions for growing a following on Pinterest.

Create A Business Account

Similar to Google+ and Facebook, Pinterest allows you to have a business profile as well as a personal profile. If you are already using your personal account for business purposes, that's ok, because Pinterest will allow you to convert your account quickly and easily.

Pay Attention To What People Pin From Your Website

If a website has had one piece of content pinned, then it is on the radar of Pinterest. As they publish a feed of pins from every website on the planet, you can already see what has been popular on your own website.

Simply type in http://www.pinterest.com/sourceand put your domain name at the end.

Now that you have your business account set up, see who has previously pinned your content and make sure you follow them.

You can also do this search for all of your competitors websites as it will give you an excellent idea of who to follow.

Pinterest also has the ability to leave comments, so you can engage with people who have pinned your content by thanking them for their pin, ask them what they like, and what they would like to see more of.

To take things a step further, you can look at what Pinterest users have pinned for your competitors and look to replicate that sort of content on your own board.

Have Multiple Boards With Their Own Themes

The most successful companies on Pinterest have at least fifteen boards that they pin to regularly. You don't need to start with this many, but categorizing the types of content you pin into different segments makes it easier for fans and for search engines like Google. Sometimes a Pinterest board that is well targeted can rank highly in search results.

An example would be if you have a shoe store, you could have a different board for each brand of shoe you sell.

You could then expand that to include boards showing customers happy with their purchase or boards that inspire. Let your imagination run wild.

Pin Regularly

Pinterest is very similar to Twitter in respect to the lifespan of a pin. As they stay relevant for only a short time, ensure you stay in the forefront of your customers minds by pinning at least once per day.

Choose From Several Sources To Pin From

Just like Facebook and Twitter, Pinterest is about both giving and receiving. It's very unusual to see an account become popular on social media without giving.

Keep a close eye on both business and personal accounts that you want to notice you. By commenting on content they pin, repinning content they add, or most importantly pinning content from their website to your board, these people will get to know you.

Pinterest sends notifications to account owners when you complete the above actions, which is a sure fire way to know they have seen your interaction.

Create A Foursquare Business Account

Another way to take advantage of multiple platforms is to make sure you are on Foursquare. In 2013 Pinterest and Foursquare created an integration called 'Place Pins', so make sure you set up your venue on Foursquare so it can be found easily on Pinterest.

Use Place Pins

While the research into the full benefits of the Pinterest-Foursquare deal is still ongoing, make sure you tag the location of your business on every photo you pin from your website.

You can also include maps on your boards by simply updating existing pins with your business location.

Maps make specific locations easier to find, so use them to your advantage and make it easier for people to find your business.

Watch And Learn From Successful Accounts

1. Perch Furniture make custom sofas in Portland. They showcase incredible interiors that inspire current customers and entice future customers.

2. Genuine Scooters have done an excellent job of using Place Pins to identify previously unknown locations in their local area.

3. WeddingWire are similar to Yelp, but for the wedding industry. They have combined geo-tagging and interesting places to get married to make a Pinterest board of highly desirable venues for the bride and groom to be.

Finally, there are many other resources at your fingertips that are designed to help you get the most out of Pinterest.

1. Pinterest have their own 'Best Practices for Business Accounts' page that is full of tips.

2. Avalaunch Media are one of the best small business marketing firms in the United States when it comes to Pinterest. Check out their blog for some great ideas.

3. TailWind is a free app you can use to refine your pinning strategy as well as analyze your followers.

Find Your Local Audience On Google+

There are currently over 350 million users on Google+ which makes it the newest competitor to try and take some of the market share from social networks such as Facebook, Twitter, LinkedIn and Instagram. However, don't let the numbers fool you.

While 350 million users sounds like an impressive figure, research shows that only 2% of social sharing happens on Google+. This is significantly less than the 50% that occurs on Facebook, 24% on Twitter and 16% on Pinterest.

Google+ is an essential part of Google's strategy to have a central login system for all of their services such as Gmail, YouTube, Play Store and general searching with the social aspect being used more as a tool for Google to track user behavior across a broader range of websites.

From an SEO perspective there are some great social media tactics you can implement, however for most small businesses Google+ should not be the sole platform used to drive social engagement.

Use Google+ As Your Business

As we know, Facebook allows you to have both a business page and a personal page. Google+ uses the same method.

Sign into Google+ with the account you used to claim your Google+ Local business page. On the top right-hand side of the page you will see a dropdown which shows you all the pages you're an administrator on.

All you need to do to use Google+ as your business is choose the name of your page from the dropdown, and Google will take you straight to that page.

When it does, Google will then show the icon for the page in the top right corner rather than your personal profile photo.

Add Your Customers To Your Circle

Facebook calls it friending, Twitter calls it following, Google+ calls it circling.

While individuals can +1 business pages or content they like, it's not possible for a business to +1 an individual. However, business pages can add individual users to circles, which is highly recommended.

A +1 on Google+ is similar to a 'like' on Facebook or 'favorite' on Twitter.

Create A Hangout Or Public Conversation

Google+ can be a great platform to host a one-to-many conversation as it integrates seamlessly with Gmail. It also removes the time-sensitive nature of tweets as Google's notification tray means participants can join your conversation on their time schedule. The chats are in a single-thread, which aesthetically makes them easier to read than Facebook posts which often fill up with frivolous comments.

Public hangouts are perfect for those in the business-to-business space as often niche industries such as accounting receive highly specific questions that can't be answered on Facebook or Twitter.

In this space video chats are an excellent way to position yourself as the authority in your industry as they can be saved and uploaded to your YouTube channel, then embedded into your website.

Participate In Business-To-Business Reviews

A lot of local business owners and employees participate in their local community through meetings and forums. People at these meetings regularly refer businesses within their community and will vouch for fellow members.

You can replicate this referral process on Google+ by completing reviews.

Using the steps mentioned above in 'Use Google+ As Your Business' start by logging in as your business.

The second step is to go to the Google+ page of the business you would like to review or recommend. To do this, go to https://plus.google.com/localand search for businesses you know. Once located, just click the pencil icon and start writing your review. Once finished, enter your rating for their business and click **'Publish.'**

Google will then ask you if you would like to share your review. The answer is 'yes', every time. Particularly if you personally know the owner of the business you have just reviewed.

Making sure the business you reviewed knows about it means they will be more likely to give you a review on Google+ as well.

You can find success by using business-to-business reviews in any industry but this technique often sees the best results in the retail or hospitality space as often these businesses refer visitors to top local attractions anyway.

Link Your Business Website To Your Google+ Author Profile

You may have noticed a smiling face next to certain search results on Google from time to time. These appear because the owner of the website has implemented something called 'authorship'.

Implementing authorship can be a complicated process, however it can lead to massive SEO gains for websites that use it because research has shown the images increase the click through rate of searchers.

To implement authorship, you need to embed a piece of code that links the page to the Google+ profile of the author of the content as well as the author of the content linking from their personal Google+ profile.

Make Sure Google+ Is Right For Your Business

As with Pinterest, Google+ isn't for all businesses. However, if your industry is something you can promote visually through videos and photos or engage in small group conversations with current or prospective customers then you should certainly look at investing some time on this platform.

Google are the giants of the search engine industry, and participating on Google+ will certainly help your SEO ranking.

The Best Of The Rest For Customer Engagement

Facebook, Twitter, Pinterest, and Google+ are the biggest hitters in social media, however there are hundreds of other social platforms you could spend time and money on, so you need to concentrate your efforts on engaging with your customers on their chosen platforms.

Let's now take a look at the second tier of social sites that can drive more business your way if you engage with people properly.

Foursquare

Foursquare is similar to Facebook when it comes to 'checking in' as it is a social network that is all about location.

Users who follow their friends on Foursquare receive an update when their friends check into a particular destination such as a bar or restaurant. Check ins are often accompanied by a photo.

To sign your business up for Foursquare visit http://business.foursquare.com.

As we detailed earlier, the Foursquare database is utilized by Instagram and Pinterest, making it essential to join even if you don't think you will actively use it.

Your business has the opportunity to leverage the free exposure offered by Pinterest and Instagram as users are prompted to add the location the photos were taken when they post on these sites.

After you create an account you will also be able to post content such as photos to your page, highlight special offers or events, and offer rewards to loyal or first-time Foursquare customers.

Instagram

There are more than 60,000,000 people using Instagram in the United States alone, and thanks to peoples love of all things celebrity this number is growing rapidly every day.

Instagram is owned by Facebook, and there is the ability to link a Facebook page to an Instagram page to post on both platforms simultaneously.

This won't come as a shock to anyone, but obviously the best ways to attract more followers to your Instagram account are to post high quality photos, to post often, and to use popular hashtags.

LinkedIn

Approximately 90,000,000 Americans are already using LinkedIn personal accounts as these days networking with your industry peers is becoming more and more important. However not many people understand the importance of creating a company page for their business.

Having a company page allows you to set up a hub for current employees where you can add photos of your business, let other LinkedIn members know about your business, and give prospective employees a better understanding of how your business operates.

Using your personal page to interact with group pages for your industry can also be a great way to raise your profile amongst potential clients. As with all social media platforms try not to spread yourself too thin by participating in too many groups and avoid answering questions with a sales pitch.

Q&A Websites And Online Forums

Q&A websites and forums aren't known as a traditional social media platform however there is a distinct advantage to being active in them.

Often the people asking the questions are potential customers, and your business can be the one that solves their problem. It also positions you as the local expert in your field.

A popular answer will also often come up in search results well after the time the question was asked.

Some popular Q&A websites and forums are:

1. Quora. This is a great site for entrepreneurs to ask a wide range of questions or to seek advice on running their business.

2. Yahoo! Answers. A site similar to Quora but used more by the general public for everyday questions.

3. TripAdvisor. The go-to place for all travel related questions and reviews.

4. Industry forums. Research your niche. Accountants use Intuit, the legal industry uses Avvo.

Which Social Network Is Best For My Business?

It's simple. The best social networks for your business are the ones your current customers already use or the ones your prospective customers are likely to be on.

It's not essential to be on every single platform, and it's important not to get bogged down spending too much time or energy on them either.

You may only need to be on two or three platforms to get the best return on your time investment.

Take things slowly based on what feels right for you and what you have time to put into running.

CHAPTER 8

Setting Up Your Website For Local Marketing—And How To Get More Foot Traffic!

For the internet, a brick and mortar outfit is no different from an online business.

This is because SEO does not discriminate; it has the same standards for all entities on the web.

The great thing about local search is that it can help your business grow its client base by targeting online users who maybe looking for the product or service you offer.

Your website, blog and brand name form the core of your digital identity, and in that order. To create a credible presence online, you need to think about your website first and foremost.

Social media activity, local business listings and email direct marketing campaigns pointless without a solid and user-friendly website.

Let's look at the basic elements of creating a webpage that means business.

At the heart of the long-term success of your website are the following four factors:

- Content - remember what Bill Gates said "content is king"
- The architecture of your website
- User-friendliness - do people enjoy dealing with your online persona?
- Technical considerations

#1. "Content Is King"

Irrespective of the online marketing channel you use, it is great content that forms the basis of success on the web.

The quality of what you put out there is the one determining factor of how your users engage with you. Keywords play a crucial role in keeping your online identity relevant.

It is no secret that most small business owners are great at creating contacts through networking events. It is easy to talk to people face-to-face about how you can help them and how what you have on offer will make their lives easier.

Writing about these features, on the other hand, is a challenge.

First, most small business owners are short on time. There is a lot to do in very little time and so online content gets put on the back burner.

Also, not everyone is a wordsmith. When all you have is the written word it becomes difficult to describe what you do to an online community.

But here is a little known fact - you do not need to be Shakespeare to write content. In fact, keep it simple; leave it a little rough on the edges. This is exactly what will make you sound authentic.

Not only this, jargon and marketing language can be off putting. Even with the more sophisticated content, you mean not win your customers over if you are unable to answer their questions about your company.

Having said that, there is no excuse for not getting the basics right.

Let's look at the main things that are required in creating great content.

- Think about what your customers are looking for
- Do you research on keywords
- What are the top questions that your customers asking?
- What sets you apart from the rest?
- Case studies
- Testimonials

What are the top things users look for?

This is perhaps the simplest and most interesting aspect of content.

In fact, you could try a little experiment right now - use Google or Bing to do this. Type any term in the search engine, and then look at the related terms that appear.

These are the most popular words or phrases in relation to what you typed. Repeat this for several terms and what you will come up with is a list of items you could include on your website in terms of content.

Use Google Trends

To hone in on what users are looking for, Google trends can provide you with some more specifics. You can look at how often people are searching for certain keywords.

Want to really zero in?

Zoom into a particular geographical location and find out which phrases are popular in those areas. Also take into account Google's suggestions regarding keywords.

What do your customers want to know?

Are there any face-to-face queries that you get on a regular basis?

Chances are, your customers are probably asking the same questions online.

For each question, try to dedicate at least a full page on your website. This will increase your chances for appearing in a search.

What is unique about your business?

From an SEO perspective, creating an area-specific for each region you operate in is a smart move. For example, if you are an electrician who works in the north of the city and intend to grow your clientele to other parts of town, you should consider including content that relates to the electrical set up in that particular region. Including a list of properties that have a history of power-related issues may also help.

Essentially, create a "local feel" for the page. The more area specific a website comes across as, the higher its chances of being rewarded by search engine algorithms.

Showcase Your Work

There is nothing more satisfying than a job well done. If you have a portfolio of work that can be showcased on your website, then by all means do so. Make sure your case studies relate to the particular geographical area that you want to grow your business in.

However, try to sound as genuine as possible - avoid sounding like an infomercial and keep it natural. You want to tell a story so visitors to your website can imagine what it is like to use your services as a customer.

The Power Of Testimonials

Content is a broad term these days, video is fast becoming a popular form of it. This is why a video recorded testimonial from your customers could work wonders not only for your website, but also for your business.

Again, it does not need to be professionally shot footage-use your smart phone and record your customers raving about your business. Simply upload this video on to YouTube and embed the link on your website. To make the most of it, include transcript of the audio. This will truly get rewarded by search engines.

#2. Site Architecture

As is evident from the term, site architecture is the way your website is organized. It relates to the order your pages are arranged in. For long-term success organize your site in a way that both search engines and visitors can understand the logical hierarchy of your content.

To make sure your website is easy to navigate, adhere to the following:

- Assign keywords and phrases to each page

- Feature and link to key content from your landing page
- Remember to include crucial content in primary navigation
- Cross link with important pages
- Have location specific pages

Let's look at each category in detail:

Assign Keywords And Phrases To Each Page

Use headlines and title tags to your advantage. By including key phrases you will attract search engine attention. Customers, too, will get a feel of how relevant your website is related to their query.

Also remember to use images that create a relevant impression of your business.

Be specific and focus on keywords so algorithms can boost your ranking.

Feature And Link To Key Content From Your Landing Page

Highlight your best feature. Just as you would in your physical outlet, make your top products stand out on the web as well. You can do so by making them a prominent element on your landing page.

Showcasing your bestsellers has a visual impact on those who visit your page. It also gets rewarded by search engines, which are constantly crawling websites. Linking deeper into your website via the landing page is we more beneficial than one content page linking to another.

If It's Important, Put It In The Primary Navigation

Search engines like Google and Bing process navigation just as a human would.

If something is in your site's primary navigation, it will get attention whether it is a real person on your website or a bot crawling it. What is not there will be ignored.

So make sure that your flagship products and contact us page can be accessed from your primary navigation link and/or drops down after a user hovers over the primary link.

Pepper Your Website With Some Cross Links

It is essential to link important pages to your content. Research shows that search engines reward content that has relevant words and phrases hyperlinked to other sections of your website. For example, a small up-market boutique could link the words "look stylish" to its latest collection page.

The idea is to create content that anticipates customer needs and gives your website credibility.

A Dedicated Page For Each Location

If there is one thing that Google rewards it is an authoritative page that contains a name, physical location and a phone number. Furthermore, include your business hours and the directions to your location.

The more you zoom in to the specifics, the higher the likelihood of your page appearing in local and mobile searches.

#3. Make Your Website User-Friendly

Spending time and energy coming up with marketing initiatives to get people to your website is all well and good - but the all important question is: are you able to convert users into customers?

There are ways to enhance user experience so you can convert the clicks to sales. Here are a few of them:

- focus on mobile searches
- make sure your contact information appears top and bottom of each page
- clear headlines
- focus on images and subheadings - text is not that important
- each page should have a purpose

Here is more information about each of these tips.

Creating A Mobile Friendly Website

More than half of all users who perform mobile searches are looking for local content. This could mean our raft of things including information about a product or service, upcoming events, news, weather and directions to get to a business location.

For a local company this statistic means that around 30 per cent of the visitors access your website using a mobile platform.

This means you need to optimize site for mobile. So you need to be mindful of the following:

- Your website should be quick to load
- It should correspond to the size of your user's screen
- Appropriately-sized buttons and links
- Include whitespace so pages readable on mobile devices

A quick note about loading time - Imagine visiting a shop where you don't get attention from the customer service staff. That is what a slow website feels like. Just as you would walk out of a business that takes long to respond to you, users leave a web page that is not quick.

Clearly Visible Contact Information

Research shows that most mobile users perform searches to look for contact details. For desktop users, you want the same level of ease when it comes to looking for your contact information.

This can be achieved very simply by making your phone number and physical address visible on each page. After all, what is the point of creating a digital identity if you cannot make it easy for people to contact you in the real world?

Use Headlines to Let People Know They're at the Right Place

The beauty of search is that people can reach specific pages on your website in a number of ways.

In actual fact, a relatively low number of people access pages within your website through the homepage. Most of them will arrive to a certain page directly because they would have entered a search query that relates to the page. Therefore, it is essential to have clear and understandable headlines. Broad terms like "welcome" or "products and services we offer" will simply not do.

Focus On Visuals and Subheadings

Research shows that most people scan through content. While it is important to keep text accurate, it is not what will engage your visitors. So, think about images to help users get an idea of what is on offer.

It is best to break the monotony of text with regular subheadings and images. After all, you have very little time to connect with your visitors, don't waste this opportunity.

Page With A Purpose

Think long and hard about what you want your visitors to gain from accessing each page on your website. Design content with that purpose in mind, when you do so, a call to action will flow organically.

For example, if you want to generate leads from your website you could say something like "contact us today". You should also make sure that the call to action is clearly visible on the page.

#4. Consider Technical Aspects

Google has a big hairy audacious goal - it wants to "organize the world's content".

Together with Bing, it has created spectacular tools within the world of search.

Nonetheless, there are some businesses that inadvertently end up designing their website in a format that is not favored by Google and/or Bing.

Here are some tips to make your site technically sound when it comes to the search engine ranking system.

- Your website should be indexable
- Your website should be crawlable
- sign up for Google analytics and Webmaster Central
- use HTML code for basic contact details
- optimize your website for mobile
- Link your Google+ author profile
- redirect your web crawlers properly

Is your site indexable?

Simple oversights and weird coding errors sometimes prove a stumbling block for search engine crawlers.

There is an easy way to check if your website is crawlable - search either Google or Bing with Site:<<insert your domain here>>.com

It is the number of pages from your website that the query returns that will help you determine if your website is well-indexed.

If pretty much all the pages from your website come back in the results you were doing well. However, if the results are scanty your website is not indexed correctly.

Now look at the blue links and the bits of text that come up. These represent the title tags and meta descriptions for each page, the two key elements of search engine optimization.

For each page you should have a distinctive headline and meta description. Make sure it is keyword optimized for the product or service that you sell as well as the location(s) your business operates from.

Checking For Crawlability

The next step should be to check if the search engine can return all the pages on your website.

To do this, run a search for each page. This can be done by searching for cache:<<insert domain name>.com/<insert page name>

On the top right-hand corner make sure you select text only version. This will give you an idea of what search engines can identify when they crawl through the pages on your website. Adding keywords creates a great opportunity for the crawlers to spot your website as a high ranking one.

Sign up for Google Analytics and Google Webmaster Central

To track how many users come to your website and what their behavior is once they're there. Check out Google Analytics - this is a free service, which is extremely handy. Analytics is a science on its own, a great starting point would be to insert a little code snippet on every page of your website. This will tell Google about your users.

Another free service from Google is Webmaster Central. This free portal alerts you to any major technical issues with your website. You can use the interface to upload a site map, which is a list of all the pages available on your website.

Arguably, they are relatively more useful for more complicated websites with a number of pages. However, small websites can also temporarily benefit from it if there are crawlability issues.

Using HTML For Basic Contact Information

An abbreviation for your business' name, address and telephone number is NAP.

It forms your digital thumbprint. Giving NAP a central position on your website will help Google associate this with the rest of your web presence. This will really help your rankings.

If it is an embedded in an image, then it is highly unlikely that it is indexable. To check this, select the characters on your NAP if you can highlight them one at a time you're in good shape. However, if you end up selecting it all in one click then it is an image. Rectify the issue immediately to help your rankings.

Optimize For Mobile

Search engines reward websites that have pages that can be easily navigated, loaded quickly, have minimal amount of code and contain images that correspond to the users' download speed.

Incidentally, these are also attributes of a mobile friendly website.

To assess how your website performs, try Google's free Page Speed tool. It is extremely helpful in identifying the elements that reduce the speed at which your website loads. It will also give you suggestions on how to increase download speed.

Link To Your Google+ Author Profile

"Authorship" is a great way to get clicks. You can do so by embedding a simple piece of code that links a page on your website to the Google+ profile of the person who wrote the content. The author ,too, can link to your website from his Google + profile.

What this results in is a picture of the author next to the search results. Research shows people are more likely to click on pages that have an image associated with them on the results page.

Redirect Web Crawlers To The Latest Information

Even though certain pages may not be visible to users because you have updated them, Google still has a record of these.

Without instructions to the crawlers to revise the index to reflect the updated information, you are likely going to be penalized. This is because sometimes when a user enters a query, the search engine could return the older version of a page, hence creating a sub optimal user experience. Later down the track this is likely to affect your website rank.

As you've probably noticed, more and more people are using smartphones and tablets to do everything they used to do on their computers – such as shopping, paying bills, checking email, and engaging in social media.

Due to this, mobile marketing has given businesses around the world a new way to connect with local consumers; right on their mobile devices.

Smartphones and tablets are the two primary types of devices used for mobile marketing, and each offer unique advantages and challenges. At their core, however, both devices utilize the same types of marketing.

Advertising is a field that has grown alongside technology. Marketing was primarily done on the radio in the early to mid-1900s, mainly on television in the mid-1900s to the present, and so on. As technological advancements have led to the evolution and creation of new mediums, marketing methods and requirements evolved.

Mobile marketing is extremely similar to Internet marketing, but with all the focus being on reaching consumers via their mobile devices. Instead of trying to air commercials during times when their target demographic is active, such as with television and radio marketing, mobile advertisers must have a different approach.

For instance, they have to look at a myriad of aspects including network coverage, the types of smartphones or tablets being used by their target market, audience segmentation, and much more.

In addition to the added complexity, however, mobile marking also provides increasingly accessible and effective advertising possibilities.

Are you still wondering if mobile marketing is right for your company?

Taking the plunge into mobile marketing is somewhat scary for a lot of businesses, which is understandable. However, you can no longer afford to ignore this massive opportunity to truly get in front of your target market.

Mobile marketing is a very broad term and can be somewhat confusing. Here are some of the top questions most businesses have about mobile marketing; this should help clarify some things that you may have been wondering about yourself:

1. What is a Mobile Website?

In a nutshell, a mobile website is a website that is easily viewable from mobile devices, such as smartphones and tablets. Traditional websites were made for viewing on desktop computers. However, these pages are not easily accessible from mobile devices.

Mobile phones and tablets do not have the processing power, large viewing screens and fast speeds of desktop computers. So when mobile users access the web via their mobile devices, they usually experience slow loading speeds as well as the inability to find the information they need due to the amount of excessive scrolling that is required.

Therefore, businesses should have a mobile-friendly version of their websites, which still consists of browser-based HTML pages. However, these pages are built to comfortably fit and view on mobile devices that access the using WiFi, 3G or 4G networks.

Mobile websites also allow users to access mobile-specific features such as click-to-call, click-to-email, or location-based mapping.

Businesses that want to capture their mobile audience must consider adaptability so their websites are compatible with all mobile operating systems; this includes being navigable through multiple browsers and visible at all mobile resolutions.

2. What is a Mobile App?

The mobile app industry is exploding and expected to be a key player in the marketing world. Mobile applications, also called "mobile apps," are software applications that have been created for small handheld devices, such as smartphones and tablets.

Most mobile devices today come pre-loaded with multiple apps and consumers can download many more via the internet; these apps can be found through various application distribution platforms.

Mobile apps range in size and complexity to fit the overall goals of the business. These apps are created to allow instant, real-time interaction with your customers; this includes making special offers and promotions directly to them via their mobile devices.

Some common app features businesses use today are social media and blog integration, mobile coupons, push notifications, ordering and reservations, list-building features, and much more.

3. What Is The Difference Between a Mobile Website And a Mobile App?

Mobile websites and apps can seem very similar at first-glance, but they are totally different. Determining which is best suited to fit your needs depends upon a number of factors, including the make-up of your target audience, your available budget, how you plan to use them, and required features.

If possible, it's not a bad idea to get both if they fit your goals and budget; the more mobile exposure you have, the better. Generally speaking, mobile websites are regular sites that have been streamlined and optimized for mobile use. The display and functionality on mobile devices and mobile apps are often used in a complimentary role.

For instance, a delivery restaurant, which offers online ordering from their main website might offer the same functionality in a stripped down fashion for mobile users.

They will likely eliminate most bandwidth-intensive images and only include a basic menu instead of one with in-depth descriptions of each dish. The goal for mobile websites is to give the user the basic functionality of your main website while compensating for mobile limitations.

If that same restaurant had a mobile app, as well, users might expect to find deeper descriptions of the types of food they sell, or other information relating to the food, region, or restaurant itself.

Mobile apps are not intended or suited to be a replacement for a mobile website due to the fact that the end goal is different for both.

4. What is Text Message Marketing?

This marketing method is relatively simple and consists of exactly what it sounds like: marketing to individuals via direct text messages. Since it is illegal to indiscriminately harvest thousands of phone numbers and send unsolicited messages, those wishing to engage in this type of marketing require interested consumers to sign up for it voluntarily.

Once signed up, consumers receive periodic text messages informing them about special offers or sales, for instance. Text messages are effective tools to send directed messages to interested people; the only potentially hard part is getting those people to take the steps to sign up. Once they do, most of them become loyal customers who look forward to receiving messages about your offers; which equates to more repeats sales and higher profits for your business.

5. What is a QR Code?

QR codes (Quick Response), are the little black barcodes you may have seen on printed advertisements and products, such as magazines, flyers, and even websites. Users with capable smartphones can install barcode apps and then scan and read those codes.

QR codes can direct users anywhere on the web, from your main business website, to a sale page, to mobile-exclusive coupons, to online videos and more. While only a small percentage of the total mobile market has scanned QR codes to date, that number is growing quickly.

Businesses all over the globe are starting to use these codes to build excitement around their company by providing instant gratification to mobile users.

6. What is In-App Advertising?

Many non-business related apps, such as text message apps, maps, games, and others, offer advertising space within their apps. If a business's target audience plays a particular game more often than others, that business can potentially pay for a banner ad to display to app users.

This method requires much of the same research as actual website advertising with the added consideration of whether the app in question actually offers ad space.

7. What Do I Need To Know About Smartphones and Tablets?

Since smartphones have effectively become miniature, portable computers that have vastly more functionality than older style cell phones, it helps to know which type your target demographic uses more because your marketing strategy will vary greatly depending on the answer. Different types and brands of smartphones and tablets are more popular among different demographics.

For example, Apple products are highly popular among younger people who live in urban environments, and Android-powered devices are rising in popularity within that and other demographics at an ever-increasing rate. Blackberries are more popular amongst the older, business crowd. Each type presents its own challenges that must be addressed:

* Coverage Area – Have a marketing strategy that depends upon a high transfer of data, such as with images or video? You want to pay special attention to the availability and speed of coverage in the areas you plan to market in. It would be a waste to create a video advertising your business, for example, only to release it an area where nobody will be able to watch it.

* Where To Market Your Mobile Presence – For those wishing to advertise with the least amount of stress and effort, major websites like Google, YouTube, Facebook, and others are popular options. They provide cheap marketing solutions for those who don't have the time or budget to thoroughly research the habits of their target demographic. For those who do decide to research into all the specifics of their target audience, the options for where you end up marketing are as varied as the demographics themselves.

8. What Demographic For Age Tends To Be The Best Target For Mobile Marketing?

As with any marketing platform, researching prime demographics is an important element of preparing for a successful campaign. At the end of the day, target demographics will depend on your business.

For instance, a local video game store will do better targeting the 18-29 age group while a local remodeling contractor may have more luck in a higher age bracket.

For those who are not interested in serious demographic targeting, the 18-29 age bracket takes first place as far as the percentage that own smartphones.

Regardless of these percentages, again, it pays to do your research to find the best age group specific to your business type.

9. What is the Social, Local, Mobile Movement?

SoLoMo, or Social, Local, Mobile, is one of the fastest growing and most prominent trends in mobile marketing today. National marketing options are wasted by local businesses that operate within a small, specific area.

Companies that provide advertising services have begun to take steps to address that problem by offering local marketing packages catered specifically for small, local businesses with limited budgets.

Companies looking into entering the mobile marketing arena are in the unique position of being able to utilize a relatively new tool that is constantly evolving and changing to meet the increasing demands of life on the go.

Most consumers engage in social media from their mobile devices, which is great for businesses that are revving up their mobile marketing efforts. By going mobile, you're essentially boosting your social presence as well.

10. What Are Some Things That I Should Research Before Starting?

Like advertising in any medium, from billboards to television to mobile, certain things need to be reviewed to ensure your marketing efforts are right for your intended targets. The primary difference between mobile marketing and other forms of marketing is that it requires a closer look at consumer behavior; and in this case, their mobile behavior.

If you are getting a mobile website, you should first figure out what type of information your audience would be looking for when accessing your site from their mobile devices. Is it directions? Is it a menu? Is it your hours of operation? It could be all of these. However, keep it simple and only provide important information they would want quick access to on your mobile website.

If you are going to start a Text Message Marketing campaign, it is important to research who your target audience is, decide on the best way to get them to opt-in to your list, and finally, decide what types of content and special offers you will be sending to them. You should also decide how often you will send messages to your list, as well as how you will track the results.

These are just a couple of examples of things you should research, but a professional mobile marketing specialist will be able to help you research and plan the right strategies for you.

While it may seem like a daunting amount of information in the beginning, internet marketing was just as complicated and involved at its inception. However, it has taken the marketing world to new places that were unimaginable just a few years ago. Mobile advances promise to revolutionize marketing just as much as the internet itself did.

CHAPTER 9

Tracking Your Local Marketing Success

Marketing your local business online provides a far easier set of methods to track and communicate advertising methods. All tech-based strategies—whether they cost money or not—and tools used for online marketing are able to generate more data than the outdated marketing methods used in the past.

This also provides a much better way to assess your company's progress, and to fine-tune your strategies to attract customers. Businesses usually rely on site analyzers and feedback from clients to collect the most up-to-date information on marketing programs and their usefulness.

There are several popular analytics tools made by various companies (e.g. Google Analytics) that help businesses see how clients and potential customers find them online. This information can then be used to discover whether a social media site, your online advertising campaign, or another web-based marketing tool worked best to attract customers.

Analyzing your web presence in this way can provide a lot more detail on what draws a client in, instead of viewing the amount of traffic on your site with no context. Specifically, these programs can track what clients have purchased or otherwise interacted with your site in more ways than a simple site visit can.

Listening to customer feedback can also greatly improve your business's customer satisfaction rate, and provides the most important role in tailoring your marketing to your clients. Customer feedback can be in many forms online, from surveys to comments on your page.

These are all important, even if the customer is dissatisfied, because it brings in specific details that simpler analytics do not. This human element of discussion is something that analytics lack, and can help your campaign fine-tune any weak elements that sheer numbers may not show.

These two crucial pieces of marketing interaction are completely free, and have the potential to give valuable information on your client base, and your targeted consumer. Feedback from customers, combined with programs such as Google Analytics can provide incomparably helpful specifics to the nature of your audience.

As if that wasn't enough, these fantastic methods of marketing analyzation are available to anyone online for free. Why not learn about your audience, and begin a road to marketing success with these easy and effective methods?

Let' Do This One Step At A Time

To effectively market a product or service, whether online or offline, time and patience are crucial elements.

With the slew of online marketing options available to businesses, getting started can seem difficult at first, even using free tools. Following these simple guides can help you and your business in several ways. Major steps to take over the course of your plan are to define your goals, to stick to a detailed plan, and start your journey to successfully marketing your plan online.

The First Couple Weeks

First things first: if your business is going to be marketed online, you need a web presence for your company. After you have somewhere for online clients to access, you can begin promoting the company through your existent web presence.

Website:

Registering your domain through a reputable site hosting company is the very first step to your online success. After you have registered a domain name, changing it can be a very complex process, so make sure your first choice is well-researched and that your site's name embodies what you want your company to be about.

All sites with multiple functions should have a Content Management System such as WordPress or Joomla, but there are a multitude of CMS outlets to choose from. These can also have systems in place to help you design your site using templates and widgets, much easier than coding the site yourself.

Online Brand Identity:

If your business is local, you can use Google or Bing Places to claim the business's location. This process could take a few days to verify, but once your business is literally on the map it will make your company much easier to locate.

Secondly, social media sites like Twitter and Facebook are completely free to create, and can help customers find you online through any site. Creating accounts on social media sites and bookmarking sites like Reddit can really boost your business's reach online quickly and without cost. Geographic location-based sites like Yelp can also help customers review your services, and can assist your local business in standing out.

Communicate and Learn from your Audience:

Seeing a competitor's audience and customer reviews can help you do better what they do wrong. Researching the competition can also bring to light various ways to reach possible clients.

Checking reviews from your competition's customers can also show who is doing what best (customer services or products). Promotional events are a great way to draw in initial customers. Offering a discount to your target audience can be a great way to draw in some first clients.

All in the Details

Pick an online payment service to assist you in collecting payment for your goods or services. One example of such a service is PayPal, currently one of the most used and easy-to-use online payment service.

Additionally, PayPal processes payment for you, so security risk is minimized. Using something like PPC can be improved by visiting Google Display Network, which can help you create various media advertisements like text and video-based ads.

The Third and Fourth Weeks

Now you've created an online footprint through your website, and you have a social media presence as well, in addition to beginning to research and connect with your audience.

The next step in your marketing strategy is active promotion. After these next techniques are put in place, you can improve your SEO while also bringing in clients to your various web presences.

Google AdWords is a great tool to pick the best keywords for your campaign. Usually sticking to 3-5 word phrases is best, and Google can help you select specific words that are both popular and competitive to your competition.

You should also begin adapting your site to be visible to various search engines and human users. Placing keywords in a non-intrusive fashion in meta tags and your site's body text can assist in SEO.

Creating a blog showing that you know what you're talking about, while also interacting with the visitors to your site can build a better relationship with clients. Post often and regularly, be it once a day or once a week. Keeping your site's posts up-to-date gives a current feel.

Definitely track your company's growth with a program such as Google Analytics. You can also take your company's web-presence to the next level by updating social media accounts like Facebook with current announcements such as products being launched, or special company events. **Market on social media often (every day if possible).**

Once you have a good idea of the audience you have, creating and publishing banner ads can give customers a quick feel for your business, as well as using landing pages as a quick impression to grab an audience from various locations.

These are key elements that can make or break a potential customer, so make them communicate how useful your product or service is!

Divide and categorize your email list of customers, so that you can give a more personalized experience to each user based on their past business or demographic. Additionally, creating an online newsletter and getting subscribers can really help your business grow.

Week 5 and Beyond

Now you have a great structure for your marketing to grow in. With these strategies in place, your company's success can be ensured through maintaining your new online presence, using a regular posting schedule, updating the content of your various sites, and keeping in touch with your audience through social media and other resources.

Always check for emails from your customers to help them with questions or concerns about their experience.

Take some time out of your day, preferably in 10-20 minute sessions, to interact and post on social media through your site's page, as well as posting any news to do with your business.

Publish blog posts often, as much as a post every day. Keep an eye on trends and the customers' habits of interaction with your business, and use this information to stay current and interesting. Create and send a newsletter once or twice a month. Only send relevant and useful information to your customers through this!

You can also boost your traffic posting to sites like YouTube, to create engaging media that attracts customers. YouTube can be used for demos, tutorials, blogs, and even reviews of your company's products or services.

Lastly, review your marketing strategy's traffic and advertisements at the end of the month to see where customers come from most. Web analytics can help a lot here, don't forget to utilize them!

Final Thoughts

Marketing a business online can seem impossible at first. But after these easy steps, you can bring your company into the online age, and improve your reach to customers.

Online marketing is a small initial investment, but the return can often be substantial. Web-based marketing is largely free, making it a great option to increase customer traffic. After completing these relatively simple steps, and keeping to the plan set out for you, it's possible to see significant results quickly.

Conclusion

Ultimately, the key is to GET STARTED NOW.

You are already a step ahead of your competitors because you have read this far; you know what to work on and how you will work on your areas for improvement.

By now, you should be able to create an effective online Local Marketing Strategy that includes a

Another key is your willingness to continue this path, and I should offer my congratulations on reaching this point – I assure you that you are a few steps ahead of your main competitors, as they are still struggling to identify their problems.

I hope that as you have reached this point, you have become aware of the importance of having a well defined Marketing Strategy that also deals with the online segment. Each element must be cleverly integrated so it can sustain and increase the importance of each other.

All the above must be completed without the necessity of having YOU to deal with all of this. Your main goal should be to take care of your business, your customers and your products/services.

Isn't that why you started your business?

Never, not even for a second, should you believe that your goal is to understand how to solve algorithms from different search engines, or any other high tech issues.

Focus on making your business function.

They key takeaways from this guide and other characteristics for having a great strategy prepared for the moment in which you are prepared to include your business in this Internet Revolution:

- Always have in mind that it is necessary to be a perfect match with your Overall Business Strategy
- Create it in such a way that it will bring in more visitors from the Internet

- It must be able to attract and collect leads that will be inserted into an Automatic Marketing Funnel that is designed to transform the leads into customers.
- You need to be able to track, quantify and improve it
- You must be 100% certain that if you decide to invest in advertising, the leads will transform into customers.
- You need to be able to measure it
- It must be able to work non-stop in a Predictable Manner
- Consider about reducing the levels of difficulty, not adding them
- It must be able to treat your visitors and customers in a pleasant manner.
- You need to include different follow ups that should be relevant, multiple targeted and even personalized. Studies have shown that a sale is conducted after 5 contacts.
- It should never need you to get involved even more

The next step you will need to follow in order to prepare your business for its imminent success. I am the first one to send you Congratulations, and more success!!!

Get a Free Gift: http://internetballyhoo.com/free-gift/

Password: FreeBallyhoo!